My Prayers

To God
with Love and Joy

Original Title: *Le mie Prime Preghiere*

© Periodici San Paolo Milano 2003
© Edizioni San Paolo 2003

English Edition
© Pauline Books & Media, 2003

Text by Bruno Forte and Antonio Tarzia

Prayers

Bruno Forte: 32, 35, 36, 39, 40, 45
Antonio Tarzia: 46, 48, 51, 52, 53, 54, 57,
59. 61, 63
Rina Risitano fsp: 42, 43

Illustrations

Raffaella Zardoni: front cover, 3, 6, 9, 10, 13, 16, 17,
19, 21, 23, 27, 29, 37, 38, 41, 44, 47, 55, 58, 62
Elaine Penrice fsp: 15, 25
Mary Lou Winters fsp: 8, 31, 33, 34, 43,
48, 49, 50, 53, 56, 60, back cover

Editor: Rina Risitano fsp
Translation: Maria Healy fsp
Design: Mary Lou Winters fsp

ISBN 0-95385 40-6-x

Pauline Books & Media
Middle Green
Slough SL3 6BS
T 0753 577629   F 0753 511809
productions@pauline-uk.org
www.pauline-uk.org

Introduction

To pray means to raise our minds and thoughts to God. Prayer helps us realise we are not alone; it gives us a sense of confidence and brings meaning to everything, even to the smallest daily jobs.

When we say the Our Father, that beautiful prayer that Jesus taught us, it is as if we join hands with children everywhere in the world making an enormous circle with our parents, relatives and people from all over the world.

As we pray we come to know that God is here for each one of us. He is generous and provides for our daily needs. He forgives us when we are uncaring or forgetful, because his love is much greater than our faults and failings.

To pray means to respect and care for the world the Lord created. He created everything, the animals, the plants, the wind and the rain and every child born under the sun and under the rainbow - the symbol of his promise of peace for all humanity.

"When two hands, even two small hands are raised in prayer they lift up the whole world".

Fr Antonio Tarzia

My Prayers

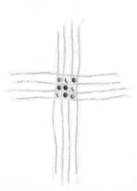

The Sign of the Cross

This prayer is a mixture of words and gestures. While we make the sign of the cross to recall the death of Jesus, we express with words our belief in the unity and the Trinity of God.

**In the name of the Father
and of the Son
and of the Holy Spirit.
Amen.**

Glory be to the Father

A prayer of praise and gratitude to the Trinity of God who creates us, chooses us as his children and surrounds us with his love.

Glory be to the Father
and to the Son
and to the Holy Spirit,
as it was in the beginning
is now and ever shall be
world without end.
Amen.

Our Father

One day the apostles asked Jesus to teach them how to pray. He replied: When you pray, pray like this:

Our Father who art in heaven,
hallowed be thy name,
thy kingdom come;
thy will be done
on earth as it is in heaven.
Give us this day our daily bread.
And forgive us our trespasses
as we forgive those
who trespass against us.
And lead us not into temptation,
but deliver us from evil.

This is the most beautiful prayer known to us. We find it in Matthew's Gospel (Mt 6:9-13).

Hail Mary

A gentle prayer to Our Lady, the Mother of Jesus. Some of the words are from the Gospel of Luke: when the angel Gabriel greets Mary at the annunciation (Lk 1:28) and at Our Lady's meeting with St Elizabeth (Lk 1:42).

Hail Mary, full of grace,
the Lord is with thee.
Blessed art thou among women
and blessed is the fruit of thy womb,
Jesus.
Holy Mary, Mother of God,
pray for us sinners,
now
and at the hour of our death.
Amen.

Angel of God

We know from the Gospels that God has given each one of us an angel to look after us (Mt 18:10). Our angel is our friend. We show our appreciation by praying to our angel.

**Angel of God, my guardian dear,
to whom God's love
commits me here.
Ever this day be at my side
to light and guard, to rule and guide.
Amen.**

Eternal Rest

When we remember and pray for those who have died it means we believe in the resurrection, that is rising from the dead. Jesus rose from the dead and when we die we too will rise with him from the dead.

**Eternal rest
grant unto them, O Lord.
And let perpetual light
shine upon them.
May they rest in peace.
Amen.**

The Angelus

This is an ancient prayer traditionally recited at midday and at 6 pm. In some countries a church bell is rung as a reminder. It recalls the occasion when the angel Gabriel told Our Lady that she was to become the Mother of God.

**The angel of the Lord
declared unto Mary.**
And she conceived of the Holy Spirit.

Hail Mary...

I am the handmaid of the Lord.
*Let it be done to me
according to your word.*

Hail Mary...

And the Word was made flesh,
And lived among us.

Hail Mary...

Pray for us O Holy Mother of God.

That we may be made worthy
of the promises of Christ.

Let us pray.

Pour your grace into our hearts, that we, to whom the incarnation of Christ your Son was made known by the message of an angel, by his passion and cross be brought to the glory of his resurrection. Through the same Christ our Lord. Amen.

Hail Holy Queen

A prayer of total trust and surrender to the motherly care of Mary, Queen of all hearts and Queen of the universe.

Hail, Holy Queen, Mother of mercy.
Hail our life,
our sweetness and our hope.
To you do we cry
poor banished children of Eve;
to you do we send up our sighs,
mourning and weeping
in this valley of tears.
Turn then most gracious advocate,
your eyes of mercy towards us;
and after this our exile,
show us the blessed fruit
of your womb, Jesus.
O clement, O loving,
O sweet Virgin Mary.

In Your Loving Care

This is the oldest prayer to the Mother of God. It is a request for help and protection.

In your loving care
we take refuge,
holy Mother of God.
Do not disregard our prayers
in the time of our need.
But deliver us from all dangers,
glorious and blessed Virgin.

The Song of Mary

Also called the *Magnificat* which is the first word of the prayer in latin, this song is in Luke's Gospel (Lk 1:46-55).

My soul proclaims
the greatness of the Lord,
my spirit rejoices in God my Saviour;
for he has looked with favour
on his lowly servant,
and from this day
all generations will call me blessed.
The almighty has done
great things for me:
holy is his name.
He has mercy on those who fear him
in every generation.
He has shown the strength
of his arm,
he has scattered the proud of heart.

He has cast down the mighty
from their thrones,
and has lifted up the lowly.
He has filled the hungry
with good things,
and has sent the rich away empty.
He has come to the help
of his servant Israel
for he has remembered
his promise of mercy,
the promise he made to our fathers,
to Abraham
and his children for ever.

The Apostles Creed

This is a summary of our Christian faith. When we recite the Creed, we express our belief in a shared common faith.

I believe in God, the Father almighty,
creator of heaven and earth.
I believe in Jesus Christ,
his only Son, our Lord.
He was conceived
by the power of the Holy Spirit
and born of the Virgin Mary.
He suffered under Pontius Pilate,
was crucified, died and was buried.
He descended to the dead.
On the third day he rose again.
He ascended into heaven,
and is seated at the right hand
of the Father.

He will come again
to judge the living and the dead.
I believe in the Holy Spirit,
the holy catholic Church,
the communion of saints,
the forgiveness of sins,
the resurrection of the body,
and life everlasting.
Amen.

The Beatitudes

In eight short sentences Jesus gives us a summary of the Good News he preached and which we find in the four Gospels.

1 Blessed are the poor in spirit, for theirs is the Kingdom of Heaven.

2 Blessed are those who mourn, for they shall be comforted.

3 Blessed are the meek, for they shall inherit the earth.

4 Blessed are those who hunger and thirst for righteousness, for they shall have their fill.

5 Blessed are the merciful, for they shall receive mercy.

Blessed are the pure of heart,
for they shall see God.

Blessed are the peacemakers,
for they shall be called
children of God.

Blessed are those persecuted
for the sake of righteousness,
for theirs is the Kingdom of Heaven.

These promises, part of the Sermon on the Mount, are in Matthew's Gospel (Mt 5:3-10).

The Ten Commandments

These are the laws God gave to Moses on Mount Sinai. They are important rules that help us relate to God and other people in a correct and just way.

I am the Lord, your God.

1 You shall have no other God besides me.

2 You shall not take the name of the Lord, your God, in vain.

3 Remember to keep the Sabbath day holy.

4 Honour your father and mother.

5 You shall not kill.

6 You shall not commit adultery.

7 You shall not steal.

8 You shall not bear false witness against your neighbour.

9 You shall not take your neighbour's wife.

10 You shall not take anything that belongs to your neighbour.

If you look in your Bible you will find these laws in Exodus 20:2-17 and Deuteronomy 5:6-21.

The Rosary

The prayer of the rosary is an easy way of meditating on the life of Jesus and Mary. While we recite the prayers we reflect on his childhood, his time of preaching, his message of light, his suffering, death and his rising from the dead, never to die again.

The Joyful Mysteries

1. The angel tells Mary of Jesus' birth. *(Lk 1: 26-38)*
2. Mary visits her cousin Elizabeth. *(Lk 1: 39-45)*
3. Jesus is born in Bethlehem. *(Lk 2: 1-7)*
4. Jesus is presented to God in the temple. *(Lk 2: 21-24)*
5. Jesus is found in the temple. *(Lk 2: 41-50)*

The Mysteries of Light

1. Jesus is baptised in the river Jordan. *(Mt 3:13-17)*
2. Jesus performs the miracle in Cana. *(Jn 2:1-11)*
3. Jesus teaches about the kingdom of God. *(Mt 5:3-10)*
4. Jesus is transfigured on the mountain. *(Mk.9: 2-8)*
5. Jesus gives us the Eucharist. *(Mt 26:26-29)*

The Sorrowful Mysteries

1. Jesus prays in the Garden of Olives. *(Mt 26:36-37)*
2. Jesus is stripped and beaten. *(Mk 15:16-20)*
3. Jesus is crowned with thorns. *(Jn 19:1-5)*
4. Jesus carries the cross to Calvary. *(Lk 23:26-32)*
5. Jesus dies on the cross. *(Jn 19:25-30)*

The Glorious Mysteries

1. Jesus rises from the dead. *(Mt 28:1-8)*
2. Jesus ascends into heaven. *(Mt 24:50-53)*
3. The Holy Spirit descends on the apostles. *(Acts 2:1-4)*
4. Mary is taken into heaven. *(Ap 12:1)*
5. Mary is crowned queen of heaven and earth. *(Lk 1:46-49)*

When praying the rosary the **Our Father** is recited after each mystery. The **Hail Mary** is repeated ten times followed by the **Glory Be to the Father**. The **Hail Holy Queen** is said at the very end.

For My Mum and Dad

Lord Jesus,
even though you are God
you wanted a mum.
Take care of my Mum,
may she be like yours,
with a heart always full of love.
Help me to appreciate always
this wonderful gift
you have given me.

Dear Lord,
remember my Dad,
he is very important to me.
Give him strength, faith and love.
Help me to grow with him
in goodness and happiness.
Help me to be kind and good
to all those who love me
and care for me.

For My Grandparents

Dear Jesus,
I am sure your grandparents
were important to you.
I love the way mine are so loving
and patient with me.
Bless them
and keep them in your love.
May I always be
a source of joy for them
and learn some of the
many beautiful things
that experience of life
has taught them.

When I Play

Dear God,
when I think of all
you have done for us
in creating heaven and earth
I feel sure you must have had
a lot of fun.
Do you like to play?
I do and I hope that when I am
at play you are with me
and enjoying yourself
as much as I do.
Help me to love
the friends I play with
and never be a bully or a show-off.
I would like to win every game,
but help me to learn
that when we play
even losing can be fun.

My School Friends

Dear Jesus,
even you went to school
when you were young.
I wonder if your friends were nice,
and sometimes horrible,
like mine.
How did you manage
to love all your friends
all the time?
Show me how and help our class
to become
a little community of friends,
where we feel happy to be together
and feel sad
when someone is missing.
Thank you, Jesus.

The Children of the World

Dear God,
sometimes when I think of
the many children in our world
I wonder how you manage
to love them all, one by one.
Yet you do, because you are God.
Help me to look kindly
on all the children I meet
and those I may never
come to know.
Because you are our Father,
they are all my brothers and sisters,
regardless of
the colour of their skin
or the language they speak.
Help me to share what I can
with those who are in need,
especially other children like me.

For My Teachers

Thank you, Lord, for my teachers,
for their kindness,
their patience and dedication.
They welcome me
and accompany me
as I learn how to live with others,
and respect everyone.
Year after year,
they help me grow in knowledge,
in skills and understanding.
Sometimes they scold me
and make me apologise
for my bad behaviour.
I don't like that,
but I know that they are right
and that they do it
because they care for me.

Dear Lord,
bless my teachers and all the adults
who care for children.
Help me to listen to them,
to be respectful and obedient.

Prayer for Studying

Dear God,
sometimes I am happy to study
because I learn many things,
but sometimes I wonder
why we were not born already
knowing everything.
It would be less troublesome!
But then maybe life
would not be so wonderful,
because very often the results
of our efforts bring great joy.
Help me to love my studies
and take them seriously,
so I can learn many things
which will enable me to be
more generous and understanding.
And when I find it hard to cope,
Lord, please be patient and help me.

Morning Prayer

Good morning, Lord!
Help me to be good today
and to avoid being naughty.
Protect me from danger.
Look after me
as I am small and defenceless
and need your protection.

Before Meals

Thank you, Lord, for our food.
Help those less fortunate than us.
Please provide proper nourishment
for all the children in our world.
Keep my family healthy
as well as all our relatives
and friends.

For Beautiful Things

Thank you, Lord,
for the many beautiful things
you give me.
For the rainbow,
a symbol of peace,
and the snow that covers the earth
like a white mantle.
Thank you for holidays by the sea
and kites that fly with the wind,
as they dance in endless space.
Thank you for Mum's smile
and Dad's warm heart.
Thank you for school, comics,
cartoons, teddy bears.
Thank you for hugs,
which I love so much.

Thank you Lord!

Thank you, Lord,
for all the food we enjoy.
May we never be without the
nourishment we need.
Help us to put an end
to hunger in the world.

Thank you,
for water, your most gentle
and precious gift.
I pray that
all the children in the world
will have enough water
to quench their thirst.

Thank you,
for sweet smelling, colourful fruit,
for nourishing milk and ice-cream
so refreshing and good.

Thank you,
for chocolate, sweets and
candyfloss,
for grandma's apple tart
and birthday cakes,
and for all the lovely sweet things
that remind me of you.

A Night Prayer

Thank you, Lord,
for this day,
for all the good things
that happened
and all the happy,
smiling people I met.
Forgive the naughty things I did
and the good things I failed to do.
Help me sleep well.
Good night, Lord.

A Computer Prayer

Thank you, Lord, for my computer
on which I can play games
and get help with my homework.
It helps me to grow
into a mature, good adult.
Like a window,
it shows me
the boundless space of the web.
Send your Angel to me,
as you did to Tobias,
to guard and protect me
against evil and harmful websites.
I pray that this human invention
will always and only be
an instrument of knowledge,
freedom and goodness.

A Prayer for the Environment

Thank you, Lord,
for the air we breathe.
Never allow it to be polluted
because of greed.
Thank you for the sea breeze
and the gentle wind
that moves the windmill
and flies our kites.
Thank you for the mist
that makes everywhere
look so mysterious,
for the clear blue sky
and the sun
that covers everything
with its warmth and light.

A Prayer for My Town

Thank you, Lord,
for my neighbourhood,
for my town
and all it offers.
I pray for the police,
for doctors, nurses
and all who look after
the health
and rights of the people.
Give them understanding
and wisdom
so that everyone
will experience respect,
care and a sense of belonging.

A Birthday Prayer

Lord, I thank you
for this special day
when I become another year older.
Thank you for my parents,
relatives and friends
who celebrate with me.
Thank you
for the precious gift
of their love
and the lovely presents I received.
Give me the joy
of being able to love them back.

As the birthday candles increase,
each new year is your gift, Jesus.
Thank you.